B IS FOR BEDU

An illustrated alphabet book

by
Fay Gabriel
Lynn Jones
Lois Cardona
Linda Horan

*Published with the support
and encouragement of*

MOTIVATE
PUBLISHING

Dedicated to the people of the Arabian desert
who shared a part of their lives with us.

Published by
MOTIVATE PUBLISHING

Dubai: PO Box 2331, Dubai, UAE
Tel: (+971 4) 282 4060, fax: (+971 4) 282 0428
e-mail: books@motivate.ae   www.booksarabia.com

Office 508, Building No 8, Dubai Media City, Dubai, UAE
Tel: (+971 4) 390 3550, fax: (+971 4) 390 4845

Abu Dhabi: PO Box 43072, Abu Dhabi, UAE
Tel: (+971 2) 677 2005, fax: (+971 2) 677 0124

London: Acre House, 11/15 William Road, London NW1 3ER
e-mail: motivateuk@motivate.ae

Directors:
Obaid Humaid Al Tayer
Ian Fairservice

© Motivate Publishing 1998

First published 1998
Reprinted 2001, 2006

ISBN 1 86063 103 7

British Library Cataloguing-in-Publication Data.
A catalogue record for this book is available
from the British Library.

Printed by Emirates Printing Press, Dubai

PREFACE

Our book is an alphabetical collection of information gathered during our visits with Bedu people. They invited us into their goat and camel hair houses, shared their time with us, and told us about themselves.

This collection of archive photographs documents a traditional Bedu lifestyle. Their nomadic culture is vanishing because the majority of Bedu now live in cities, and for this reason the scenes that are depicted here could never be captured again.

This book fulfils our need to express our admiration for Bedu ingenuity and our delight in being touched by these warm and generous people. It is written for children to read and enjoy. However, adults may also be interested in this book, which speaks of a way of life as ancient as Abraham. The highlighted words in the text have their meanings explained at the back of the book.

Fay Gabriel, Lynn Jones,
Lois Cardona, Linda Horan

ARABIA is the home of many Bedu people. The Arabian Peninsula lies between Asia, Africa and Europe. Most Arabs live in cities today. However, some people live in the vast Arabian desert. They live as **nomads,** moving to find food and water for their herds. These people of the desert call themselves 'Bedu'.

BEDU people live in the desert plains of the Arabian Peninsula. Their ancestors have lived in this area for thousands of years. They move with their tents to places where grass and water are plentiful for their herds of sheep and goats.

These nomads are handsome people with dark hair and tanned skin. They are warm and friendly people.

CHANTING together is one way that the Bedu celebrate friendship. They often gather together and clap hands and chant in turn.

The night is dark and travellers come.
     And travellers come,
     and travellers come.

Our fire burns bright to welcome them.
     To welcome them,
     to welcome them.

Pour the coffee with cardamom.
     With cardamom,
     with cardamom.

Guests bring joy to this house of hair.
     Praise be to Allah,
     praise be to Allah.

DELLAHS are the pots in which Arabic coffee is prepared. **Dellahs** have a high position in the life of a Bedu family. In the **majlis**, or sitting area of the tent, the dellah is often present, ready to serve any traveller or friend who comes to sit by the fire when visiting.

Fresh-roasted coffee beans are pounded with a brass **pestle** in a **mortar** to make a fine powder. The ground coffee is mixed with **cardamom** and water, then boiled over the fire. The spicy-smelling brew is poured from the crescent-shaped spout of one dellah into another and finally into small cups for drinking. Several dellahs are commonly used to make coffee.

EMPTY is how most of the land looks in this part of the desert. The Bedu are surrounded by flat, sandy, barren land, but they see much in this empty-looking land. At night, the sky comes alive with many bright stars, which city dwellers do not always see. Unlike the city, the empty desert is quiet and peaceful.

FOX FUR is attached to this baby's peaked
bonnet. The baby was born to a Bedu family
one cold winter. He began his life among a
warm, supporting family. The tuft of fur came from
a fox that the baby's grandfather hunted many years
ago. His mother said that the fur is worn to give the
baby courage and wisdom like the fox. She feels the
fur will keep the child safe from evil forces.

GOATS, with their long dangling ears, are essential to Bedu life. Goat hair makes the wool for Bedu homes. Goats' milk is drunk and also made into **leban** (yoghurt), and **jebneh** (cheese). Goat meat is very good to eat. When a goat is butchered, the meal will be shared with neighbouring families, because a whole goat is too much for only one family to eat, and cold storage is not available. Goats are hearty animals and can survive on the sparse growth in the desert. Because of the limited vegetation, tent clusters are placed far apart so that each family has enough space to provide adequate grazing for its herds.

The **goatherd** carries a wooden staff while tending the flock. In the vast open desert the only sound heard might be the goats' bells, and the soft 'shhhhhh, shhhhhh, shhhhhh', of the goatherd directing the flock. The goatherd might also keep the animals together by tossing small stones to prod the strays along. The goatherd can be any member of the family. At night, some herds will be penned near the tent. Young kids may be brought into the tent for protection.

'HOUSE OF HAIR' is what the Bedu call their traditional goat-hair dwelling. This house is made by the women of the family from woven goat hair.

Putting up a house of hair is a lot of work. Long strips of woven goat hair are placed side by side on the ground to form one large rectangle. The women hand stitch the edges of the strips together. After the sewing, wooden poles are placed under the heavy cloth and the roof is raised and staked with ropes. Now the house has a roof and two walls. Sidewalls are made from more strips of goat-hair cloth and stitched in place to the roof.

The house is normally divided into rooms or sections for various uses. It is versatile, and can be made large or small, high or low. In the cold months, the roof may be lowered while in hot months, it may be raised and the sides opened to the breeze. The house can be taken apart by removing the hand stitching. The strips can then be rolled into coils and loaded onto the back of a truck as they were once loaded onto the backs of camels.

IMIRA sits with her grandchild in her house of hair. She has lived either in the desert or in small desert towns all of her life.

Imira says, 'I prefer my house of hair which invites the breeze to flow through. I prefer to sleep to the tune of the wind on the silent desert.'

She says she wishes her grandchild will also know and love the peace of the desert.

LITTERS were used as saddle-like devices placed on the camel's back to transport children and the elderly during long journeys. They provided more space, and their arched frames could be covered to shade the rider.

The rider was supported in a hammock attached inside the frame for more comfort. The woman in the picture shows how a person might ride in the litter on a camel.

MASKS are worn by many Bedu women. These black masks cover most of the face, displaying only the eyes. Often the masks are made of layers of gauze-like cloth. Sometimes they are decorated with fringes, sequins, or beads. Emphasised by the mask, the eyes are outlined with a black powdery substance called 'kohl'.

19

NOSE RINGS are worn by many women of the desert. Usually the right nostril is pierced and a silver or gold ornament is worn. Stones are often embedded in the silver or gold. Turquoise is a popular stone. Women can be seen wearing nose rings while weaving, tending flocks, or visiting neighbours.

OLIEH sits in the work section of her house of hair. She sits on a **sleeping pad** as she speaks of her family and her tribe, 'We are a large tribe with many strong people. Allah has blessed us.'

Olieh raises her hand for quiet.

'Listen, listen. The men have visitors in the majlis. They may need food or drink. Ali, take dates and leban to them. Perhaps they'd like some meat and warm milk, too.'

Ali takes the food and some empty cups around the divider, which separates the house of hair into sections, to the men sitting by the fire. The rattle of the **coffee cups** as the coffee is served can be heard coming from the majlis. Olieh continues, 'It is good to have many sons and daughters.'

She raises her hand again for silence so that she can hear the voices of the men as they talk.

PATCHWORK, beautiful in its design and colour, is used by the Bedu in various ways to add more colour to the house of hair. Very long strips of colourful patchwork curtains divide sections of the house. Patchwork might cover a small baby, or stacks of bundles. Women often make patchwork by hand or sometimes with sewing machines. They take great pride in their work.

QUARMA washes clothes for the family near the house of hair. The house of hair is usually arranged in three areas or rooms: the guest area or majlis, the working area, and the private sleeping area.

Quarma lives here with her son and his wife and their children. She knows her son will always provide for her.

RAGAYA has a new baby.
She sings to her baby and
plays with him.
She says, 'Family is everything to me.
Life would have no meaning without
a caring family and without a family
to care for.'

SHEEP are herded along with goats by the Bedu. Sheep are valued for their meat, milk, and fine wool. Yarn spun from sheep wool is softer than goat hair. It is often dyed into bright colours and woven into rugs and bags of various kinds.

TATTOOS are seen on many Bedu girls and women. They are considered marks of beauty. The chin, central forehead, cheeks, and upper lip are the areas most often adorned.

The women use sewing needles to pierce the skin to bring blood. They take soot from the bottom of a cooking pot and press it into the punctures. Although the soot is black, the **tattoo** design will turn a bluish-green as the skin heals. The designs are personal choices.

UMAR wears a traditional **gutra**. This is a
large square of lightweight cotton fabric.
It is usually white, but can have a red or
black chequer-like design. The gutra is folded into
a triangle and placed on the head, secured by the **igal**,
a black cord. It can also be folded around the head in
a turban shape.

Under a gutra, a small white cap can be worn.

The gutra serves as a shield against the hot sun,
the wind, the cold, and the blowing sand.

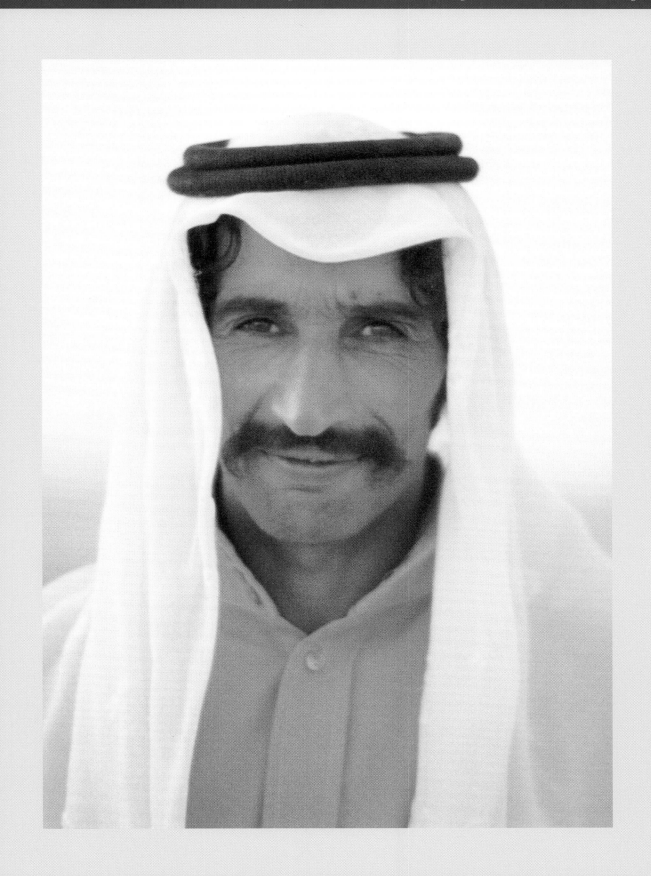

VEILS are worn by some Bedu women to cover their faces. Veils are usually black and made of a net-like cloth, light enough to see through. The veil is sometimes worn with a mask, and sometimes without. The mask is called **burghu**, and has various shapes and designs according to the tribe.

WEAVING is done with the yarn spun from the hair of goats, sheep, or camels. The loom is a simple, handmade device placed on the ground. It is made of sticks and is easy to take apart when the weaving is finished.

The designs are geometric and quite colourful. **Henna** dyes produce the orange and red colours that are often used in Bedu work. These colours contrast well with the natural brown, black, and white of the animal hair.

Sometimes weavers will purchase wool ready-dyed, and sometimes they send their homespun yarn to a city to be dyed.

The panels which divide the Bedu house of hair into sections frequently have strips woven with special designs. Decorative stripping is often used to connect the panels of the house of hair.

31

X is the shape of the top of the wooden spindle used by Bedu women to spin yarn. At the centre of the X there is a hook to catch the wool. The wool is twisted and pulled tightly between the hand and the spindle to form yarn. It takes a long time to spin enough yarn with which to weave.

YASIR is the third son of his father. His father has a large herd of sheep and goats. Yasir helps his father with the herd after school. Yasir and his brothers drive their four-wheel drive to school. Their school is about one hour away in a small village. Boys attend one school and girls attend another.

Yasir studies mathematics, reading, religion and English. He is a bright student. His mother tells him to learn everything he can. Yasir is a good son. He honours his father and mother.

ZAYNAB thinks of the past when a friend asks, 'How old are you, Zaynab?'
She spreads her arms wide and says, 'How can I know? There is no way to know. Allah is all merciful. I have lived long in his favour.

'I remember once long ago when water was so scarce that the blood didn't run when a goat was slaughtered. Those times have passed. We now have water trucks to bring water when there is no rain. **Al hamdu lillah**. There are now hospitals and schools and good roads. Life is changing. Allah will provide.'

Now find out the meanings of the highlighted words!

Al hamdu lillah: 'Thanks be to God' in Arabic.

Allah: the name for the Supreme Being in Islam.

Burghu: the mask often worn by Bedu women.

Cardamom: an aromatic seed-pod used as a spice in Arabic coffee.

Coffee cups: small ceramic cups without handles in which Arabic coffee is served.

Dellah: a coffee-pot. It is often brass with a long, crescent-shaped spout.

Goatherd: a person who tends goats.

Gutra: a white head covering worn by many Arab men. In parts of Saudi Arabia, the red and white checked head cloth is called 'shmag'.

Henna: a reddish-orange dye or cosmetic made from the leaves of a shrub.

Igal: a cord, usually black, which is worn over the gutra or shmag.

Jebneh: cheese which is made from goats' milk.

Leban: yoghurt made from goats' milk.

Majlis: the sitting area in the house of hair.

Mortar and pestle: the mortar is a brass container in which coffee beans are pounded with the pestle, a club-like instrument.

Nomads: people who move from place to place in search of pasture for their animals.

Sleeping pad: the floor covering that the Bedu sleep upon. It is a colourful layered blanket filled with padding.

Tattoo: a design or mark which is made by puncturing the skin and inserting pigment.

The publishers would like to thank Kinnarps, without whose sponsorship support and encouragement the publication of this book would not have been possible.